# COLLECTIONS

A Harcourt Reading / Language Arts Program

*Turn the page and
say hello
to new friends.*

# COLLECTIONS
### A Harcourt Reading / Language Arts Program

## YOU'RE INVITED

### SENIOR AUTHORS
Roger C. Farr • Dorothy S. Strickland • Isabel L. Beck

### AUTHORS
Richard F. Abrahamson • Alma Flor Ada • Bernice E. Cullinan • Margaret McKeown • Nancy Roser
Patricia Smith • Judy Wallis • Junko Yokota • Hallie Kay Yopp

### SENIOR CONSULTANT
Asa G. Hilliard III

### CONSULTANTS
Angelina Olivares • David A. Monti

**Harcourt**

Orlando   Boston   Dallas   Chicago   San Diego
Visit *The Learning Site!*
**www.hbschool.com**

Requests for permission to make copies of any part of the work should be mailed to the following address School Permissions, Harcourt, Inc., 6277 Sea Harbor Drive, Orlando, Florida 32887-6777.

HARCOURT and the Harcourt Logo are trademarks of Harcourt, Inc.

Acknowledgments appear in the back of this work.

Printed in the United States of America

ISBN 0-15-312034-7

1 2 3 4 5 6 7 8 9 10  048  2001 2000 99

# You're Invited

**Dear Reader,**

   **You're Invited** to meet some new friends. Join some children for a picnic. Help out a lost ant. Find out where frogs really come from. Then meet six of the silliest foxes you ever saw! Turn the page and say hello!

   Sincerely,

   *The Authors*

   The Authors

Theme **It's My Turn Now**

# Contents

# Contents

Theme

# It's My Turn Now

8

9

# Reader's Choice

### Sid and Sam

*by Nola Buck*

Two friends start singing together. One friend just can't stop singing!

**Award-Winning Illustrator**

**FROM THE LIBRARY**

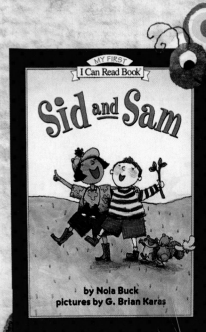

MY FIRST
I Can Read Book

Sid and Sam

by Nola Buck
pictures by G. Brian Karas

## Biscuit

*by Alyssa Satin Capucilli*

Biscuit finds that he needs a little help getting ready for bed.

**Award-Winning Illustrator**

**FROM THE LIBRARY**

## I Am Six

*by Ann Morris*

Children enjoy a day at their school.

**Award-Winning Author**

**READER'S CHOICE BOOK**

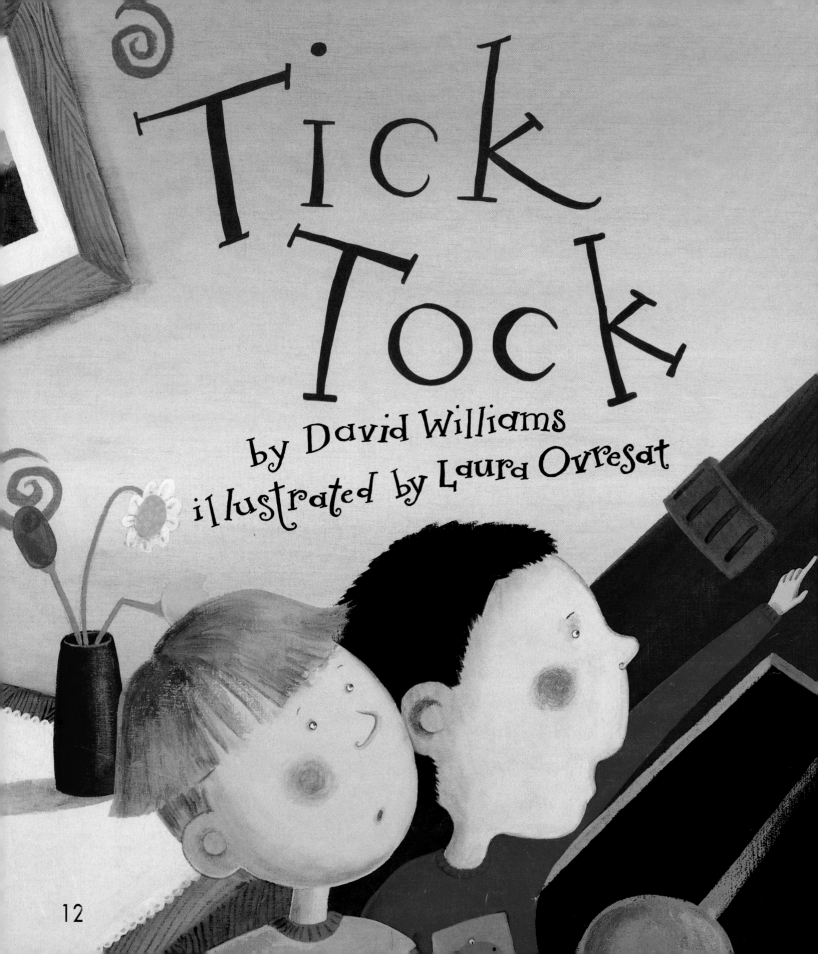

# Tick Tock

by David Williams

illustrated by Laura Ovresat

Tick, Tock!
Ticked the clock.

13

Call Kim and Mick.
We need help quick!

Pass me the mop.
We can't stop.

Tick, Tock!
Ticked the clock.

Kim picks up pots—
lots and lots!

Mick is picking up hats.
Todd is packing up mats.

18

Tick, Tock!
Ticked the clock.

Pick up that sock.
Look at the clock!

Mom's home now.
We did it. Wow!

# The Picnic

by David Williams

illustrated by Laura Ovresat

Todd, Kim,
Mick, and Rick!
Let's go on a picnic!

Toss this, toss that—
Salad for our picnic.

Pop this, pop that—
Popcorn for our picnic.

Pass this, pass that.
Pack this, pack that.

Now this is a picnic!

Walk here, walk there,
on the path to our picnic.

Hop up, hop down,
on the path to our picnic.

29

# Todd, Kim, Mick, and Rick!

Look at this big picnic!

# My Home

## Living Room

The living room is a comfortable place to relax in.

potted plant

coffee table

table lamp

rug

squishy
bean bag

soft cushion

photograph

books

flowers

reading
together

33

# Kitchen

Food is stored and cooked in the kitchen.

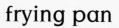

rolling pin

frying pan

cups

crisp vegetables

oven

apron

trash can

wooden
spoon

shiny
colander

saucepan

making tasty
sandwiches

oven mitt

bowl

35

# Hickory, Dickory, Dock

## Make a paper plate clock.

**1** Number a plate like a clock.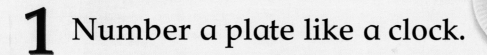

**2** Make the hands of the clock.

**3** Put the hands in the middle with a brad.

**4** Say the rhyme "Hickory, Dickory, Dock."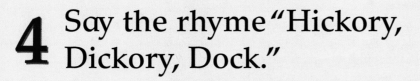

Hickory, dickory, dock,

The mouse ran up the clock.

The clock struck one,

The mouse ran down,

Hickory, dickory, dock.

37

# LOST!

Award-Winning
Illustrator

by Patti Trimble
illustrated by Daniel Moreton

"I'm lost," said Gil the ant.

"Where am I?
It's so hot in here."

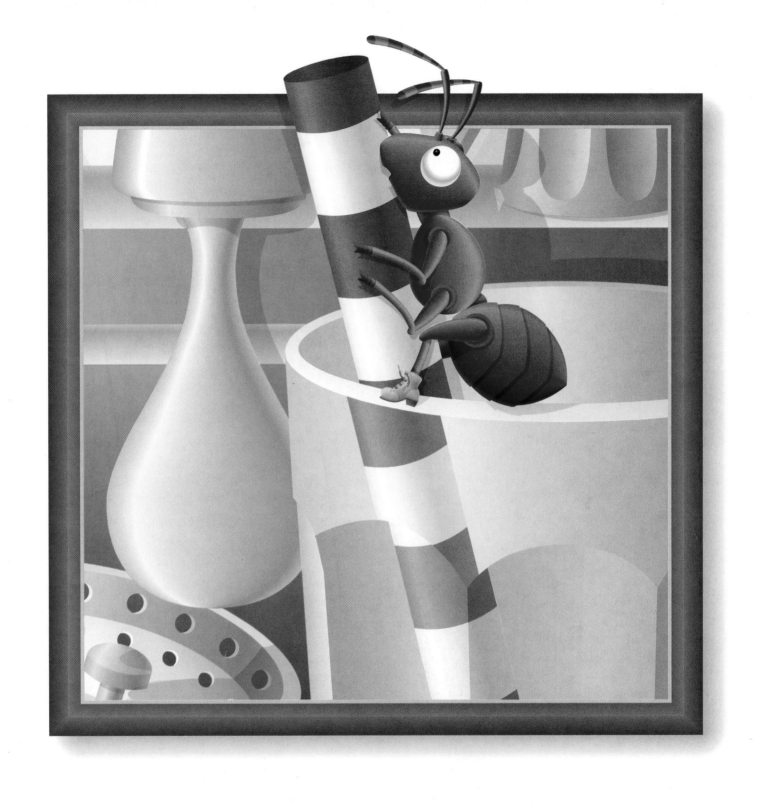

"I will walk up," said Gil.

"Now I see.
I was in a sink!"

"What is this?" said Gil.
"It's a big two."

"Oh, it's a clock!"

"Now all I see is pink!" Gil said.
"I will walk on and on."

"Oh, it's a pink mat!"

"Help!" called Gil, the lost ant.

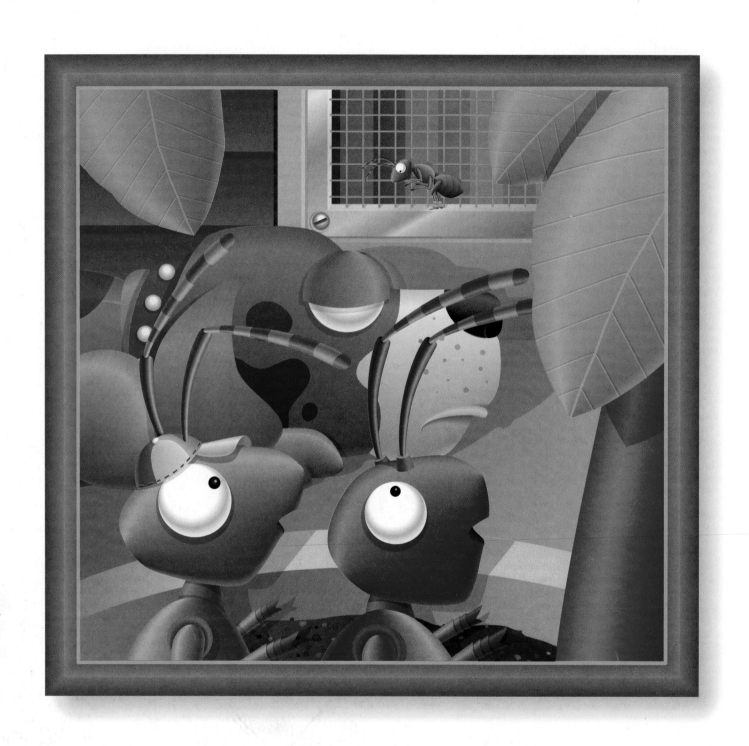

"Go past that dog,"
called his two friends.

"I'm glad to be home!" said Gil.

by Patti Trimble

illustrated by Daniel Moreton

# WHAT DAY IS IT?

Gil was glad.
"This is my big day!"

Gil saw Ann.
"Ann! What day is it?"

"It's Monday," said Ann.

Gil was sad.
"Ann forgot my big day."

Gil saw Todd.
"Todd! What day is it?"

"It's Monday," said Todd.

"Ann and Todd forgot that
this is my big day!"

Gil was so sad.
"My friends forgot."

"It's my birthday, and
they missed it."

"We did not miss it!
Happy Birthday, Gil!"

"Thank you," said Gil.
"This is a surprise!"

# ANT
## BOOKMARK

Gil lost his way.
Make a bookmark
so you can always find
where you are
in a book.

**1** Draw an ant at the top of your bookmark.

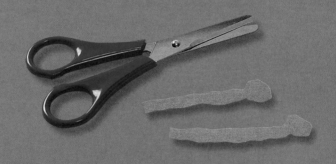

**2** Cut out two antennas.

**3** Glue them on the ant's head.

Gil is a funny ant.

**4** Write a sentence about Gil the ant.

Share your bookmark with a classmate.

# The Tapping Tale

by Judy Giglio
illustrated by Joe Cepeda

Pat ran to see Ronda.
At last, Ronda was
spending the night!

"Mom, Ronda is here."

Pat and Ronda played all day.

At last, it was time
to sleep.

"What's that tapping?"
asked Ronda.

"I can look in the hall,"
said Pat.

"Look!" said Ronda. "This
is what's tapping."

"I think it's a tail!"
said Ronda.

"Oh, that's Rip!" said Pat.
"Rip, hop up here."

"Rip is happy to see you,"
said Pat.

74

"Oh, Rip!" said Ronda. " This is better. You can sleep up here!"

# Rip's Secret Spot

by Kristi T. Butler

illustrated by Joe Cepeda

Pat could not find her frog.
"Who has my frog?"

Mom could not find her pin.
"Who has my pin?"

Dad could not find his hat.
"Who has my hat?"

Pat, Mom, and Dad looked
for the missing things.

"Pat," called Dad, "look at Rip.
He ran off fast."

"Rip is sniffing the grass.
Now he is digging."

"That dog digs all the time," said Pat.

"My hat is in that hole," said Dad.
"There is my frog!" shouted Pat.

"All our things are there! My pin is there, too," said Mom.

"I think that's Rip's secret spot!" said Dad.

"Let's dig up our things,"
said Pat.
"We will put this in the hole
for Rip!"

# Chums

He sits and begs; he gives a paw;
   He is, as you can see,
The finest dog you ever saw,
   And he belongs to me.

He follows everywhere I go
   And even when I swim.
I laugh because he thinks, you know,
   That I belong to him.

    Arthur Guiterman

Response Activity

# Guess My Pet!

You have met Pat's pet dog, Rip. Write a riddle about a pet.

**1.** Think of a pet.

**2.** Write three clues about the pet.

**3.** Trade clues with a classmate.

**4.** Read the clues.

It is green.

It eats bugs.

It is smaller than a book.

Try to guess the pet.

# Why the Frog Has

# BIG

# EYES

by Betsy Franco

illustrated by
Joung Un Kim

Long ago, all frogs had small eyes.
One frog sat and stared all day.

"No one can stare as long as I can," Frog bragged.

His friends said, "Let's stop his bragging. Who can stare as long as Frog can?"

Horse trotted in.

"You will blink first," said Frog.
"I will not!" said Horse.
"See!" shouted Frog. "You did!"

Rabbit hopped in.

Rabbit didn't last long. He blinked first. "No one is better than I am!" bragged Frog.

Fish flopped up. "Frog will blink
first this time!" said Fish.

Fish stared at Frog. Frog stared
at Fish. Fish didn't blink. Frog's
eyes got big, Big, BIG.

"Frog blinked!" shouted Fish.
"Frog, fish can't blink! Ha! Ha!"

Frog sat still. His big eyes
stared from that day on.
He didn't brag again.

# Where Do Frogs Come From?

by Alex Vern

Frogs come from
small eggs.
The black dots
on this plant are
frog eggs.

105

Pop! Pop!
A tadpole
pops out
of an egg.

Pop, pop, pop! Lots and
lots of tadpoles pop out.
A tadpole has to swim
fast or a fish could eat it!

At first, the tadpole
has a long tail and
a big body.

It looks for plants in the pond. It eats the plants and grows a lot.

Strong back legs form. They
help the tadpole kick fast
and swim. Kick, kick!

Small front legs form, too. The tadpole is now a frog that has a tail!

Now the tadpole is a big, strong frog. Its tail is gone, so it can hop.

112

Hop, hop! Plop, plop!

The frog is fast! It eats lots of bugs. The bugs were not as fast as the frog. Mmmm!

# From Egg to Frog

1. Egg

2. Tadpole

3. Frog

# FROG  CHAIN

## Make a paper chain that shows how tadpoles become frogs.

**1** Think about how tadpoles change.

**2** Draw five changes on paper strips.

**3** Make the paper strips into a chain.

**4** Share your frog chain. Tell about each picture.

# WINK'S FIRST FISH

by Rozanne Lanczak Williams
illustrated by Russ Willms

Stan had to watch
his sister for the day.

"Wink!" called Stan.
"Hop down off that wall!"

"OK," said Wink, "but first I will
sing a song."

"Up on this wall,
I am not small.
Stan thinks I will fall.
I just want to be tall."

"I want to be big like
you, Stan," said Wink.

"You will grow, Wink!"
said Stan.

"Will you sing me a song?"
asked Wink.

"OK," said Stan.

"This will not last.
You will grow fast.
Then you will be
as big as me!"

Later on, Stan and Wink saw a man with some fish. One fat fish landed on the dock.

SNAP!  Wink grabbed it.
"It's your fish now," said the man.

"That's your first fish, Wink!" said Stan.
"I will sing this song for you!"

"You are not big,
but you are fast!
This is your first fish
at last, at last!"

Wink sang back.

"I am not big,
but I will grow!
Come fish with me!
Let's go, go, go!"

# No More Fish

## A PLAY

by Hortense Carter
illustrated by Russ Willms

### CHARACTERS

Dash

Pig

Stan

Horse

Storyteller

Stan was tired of fish.

 Fish, fish, fish! That's all I eat.
I wish I didn't have to eat fish!

I am Dash! I will grant your wish.

Oh! I wish I were a horse.
Horses eat grass, not fish.

 Your wish will be granted.
PLINK!

Quick as a wink, Stan was a horse!

134

Now I will eat this grass.
Ick!

 In a flash, Dash was back.

 Why are you sad?

 I don't like grass.

Then you can have another wish.

 Oh! I wish I were a pig. Pigs eat corn, not grass.

Your wish will be granted.
PLINK!

Quick as a wink, Stan was a pig.

Now I will eat this corn.
Ick!

139

In a flash, Dash was back.

 Why are you still sad?

 I don't like corn.

 Then you can have one last wish.

I want to be a pelican again.
I miss eating fish!

 That's a good wish!

141

Quick as a wink, Stan was a pelican again!

142

I do like fish! No more wishing!
What I want to be is me!

143

Response Activity

# Our Wish Book

## What do you wish for?

**1** Write your wish.

**2** Draw a picture of your wish coming true.

**3** Put your page in a class book.

**4** Read the Wish Book.

I wish I had a bike.

OUR WISH BOOK

# Get That Pest!

by Erin Douglas
illustrated by Wong Herbert Yee

Award-Winning
Illustrator

Mom and Pop Nash had ten red hens.
Every day they got ten eggs.

One morning, five eggs were missing!

"Someone has robbed our hens!"
shouted Pop.
"We can't let him get another egg!"
said Mom.

The Nashes hid in the shed.
C-C-CRICK.
"What's that?" asked Mom.

A wolf slipped into
the shed.

He popped
four eggs
into his sack.

"It's a wolf!" shouted Mom.
"I'll get him!" shouted Pop.

"Too bad," said Pop.
"Get this net off me!" shouted Mom.

Now ONE egg was left.

"We have to get that pest!" said Mom.
"Help me set this trap."

When the trap was set, they hid.

C-C-CRICK…SMASH!
The trap got Mom and Pop.
The wolf got the last egg.

Then Mom and Pop Nash
set a BIG trap and hid.

C-C-CRICK . . . WOMP!

"Let me out," begged the wolf. "You can have all the eggs back."
"You didn't eat them?" asked Pop.

"No," said the wolf. "I PAINTED them!"

"Oh, my!" said Mom.
"Well, well!" said Pop.

Now Mom and Pop Nash sell painted eggs. Would you like one?

Painted Eggs

SIX SILLY

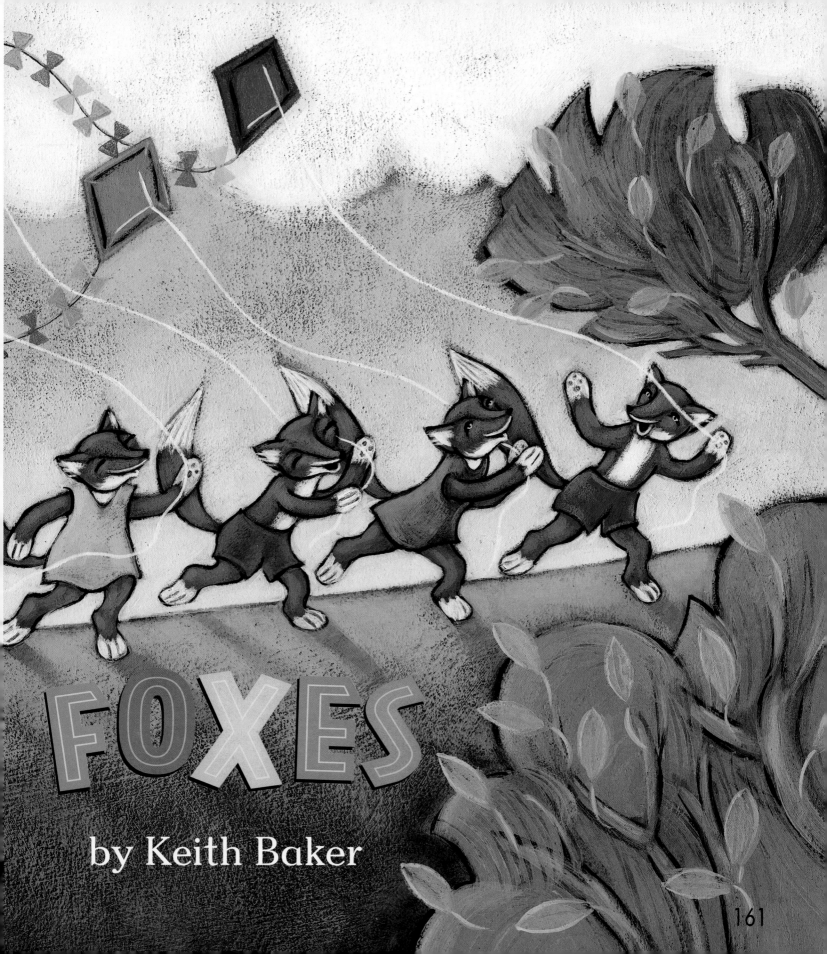

# FOXES

by Keith Baker

We are six silly foxes—
Ellen, Max, and Greg.
We are six silly foxes—
Dixon, Beth, and Meg.

How can six silly foxes
hop on boxes filled
with eggs?

We are six sad foxes.
Look at that! Oh, no!
We are six sad foxes,
very sad. It is so.
How can six sad foxes
fix an old banjo?

We are six hungry foxes,
and it's time to eat.
We are six hungry foxes
looking for a sweet.

How can six hungry foxes
snack on ice cream in the heat?

We are six mad foxes,
as mad as mad can be.
We are six mad foxes.
(Add it up—three and three.)

168

How can six mad foxes
jump into the next tree?

FOX LANE

6

170

We are six happy foxes,
very happy, you can see.
We are six happy foxes.
You ask how that can be?

Silly or sad, hungry or mad,
we are all so very happy
In this mixed-up family!

RESPONSE ACTIVITY

# THE MISSING EGGS GAME

## Play the missing eggs game.

**YOU WILL NEED**: • white paper • bag • scissors

**1** Cut out 6 eggs.

**2** Lay them in a row.

**3** Take turns being the wolf and the farmer. The farmer must not look.

**4** The wolf takes some eggs and puts them in a bag.

**5** The farmer tells how many eggs were taken.

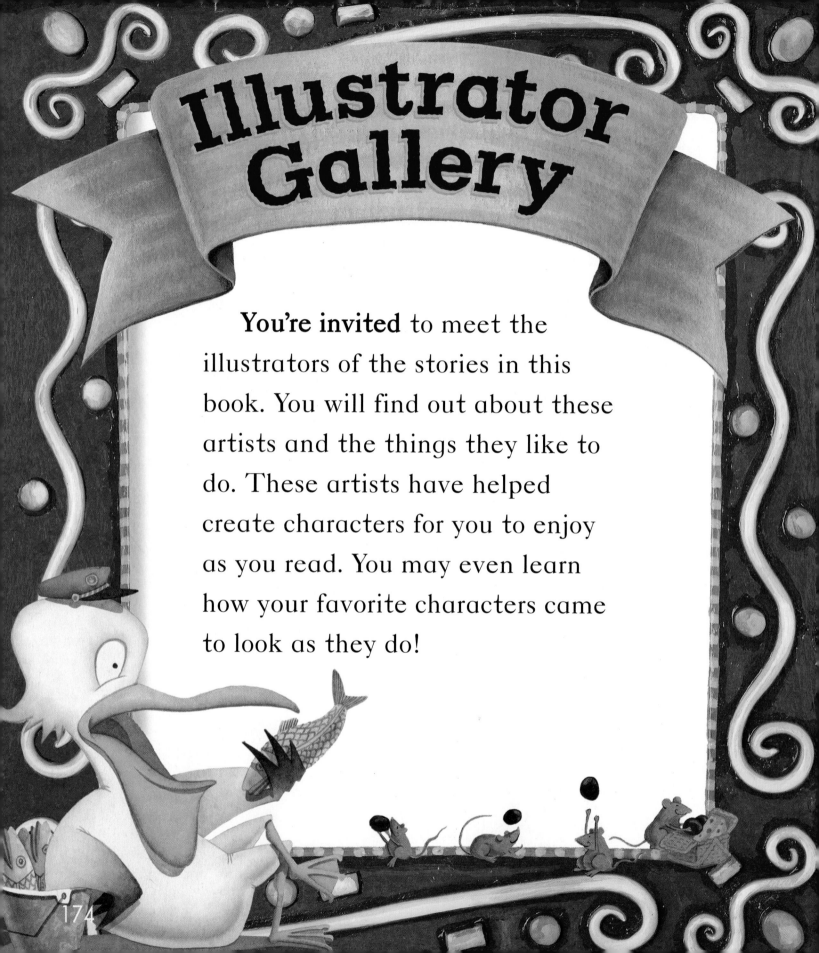

# Illustrator Gallery

**You're invited** to meet the illustrators of the stories in this book. You will find out about these artists and the things they like to do. These artists have helped create characters for you to enjoy as you read. You may even learn how your favorite characters came to look as they do!

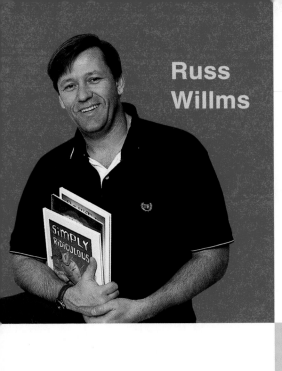

**Russ Willms**

**Laura Ovresat**

**Joe Cepeda**

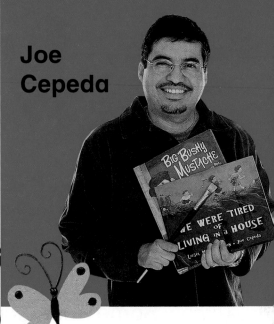

**Daniel Moreton**

**Wong Herbert Yee**

**Joung Un Kim**

**Keith Baker**

# Laura Ovresat

Laura Ovresat loves animals and the outdoors. She has been drawing animals since she was a young girl. Sometimes she likes to paint on wood instead of on paper.

*Laura A. Ovresat*

# Daniel Moreton

As a child, Daniel Moreton loved listening to his grandmother's stories. They made him want to write his own. Daniel Moreton loves to create pictures for stories, too. He uses a computer to draw them.

# Joe Cepeda

Before starting his work, Joe Cepeda reads a story many times. Then he draws the place where the story happens. He draws people last. He likes to make the characters look like people he really knows!

*Joe Cepeda*

# Joung Un Kim

Joung Un Kim visits bookstores and museums to get ideas for her drawings. She likes to try new things. For the story "Why the Frog Has Big Eyes", she practiced drawing animals. This is the second animal story she has done.

# Wong Herbert Yee

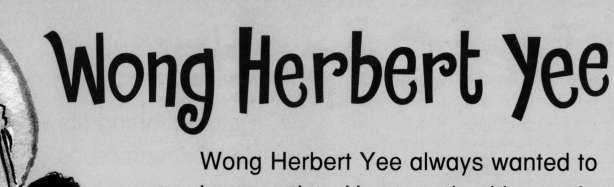

Wong Herbert Yee always wanted to be an artist. He started writing and illustrating children's books when he was an adult. His daughter is his helper. She tells him if she thinks other children will enjoy his stories.

*Wong Herbert Yee*

# Russ Willms

Russ Willms works at home in Canada. Sometimes he acts out parts of stories to help him illustrate them better. He acted out the part of the fisherman in "Wink's First Fish" to know what the fisherman would look like in the picture.

# Keith Baker

Keith Baker was a teacher before he went to art school. He writes and illustrates stories that he knows the children in his classes would have enjoyed. He says teaching was fun, but he really loves creating his own books.

*Keith Baker*

179

### Acknowledgments

For permission to reprint copyrighted material, grateful acknowledgment is made to the following sources:

*HarperCollins Publishers:* Cover illustration by G. Brian Karas from *Sid and Sam* by Nola Buck. Illustration copyright © 1996 by G. Brian Karas. Cover illustration by Pat Schories from *Biscuit* by Alyssa Satin Capucilli. Illustration copyright © 1996 by Pat Schories. Cover illustration by Barbara J. Phillips-Duke from *Digby* by Barbara Shook Hazen. Illustration copyright © 1997 by Barbara J. Phillips-Duke.

*Lorenz Books, 27 West 20th St., Suite 504, New York, NY 10011:* From *Let's Look At: My Home* (Retitled: "My Home"). © 1997 by Anness Publishing Limited.

*Louise H. Sclove:* "Chums" by Arthur Guiterman.

*Silver Burdett Press, a division of Modern Curriculum, Inc., Simon & Schuster Education Group:* Cover photograph by Nancy Sheehan from *I Am Six* by Ann Morris. Photograph copyright © 1995 by Nancy Sheehan.

### Photo Credits

Key: (T)=top, (B)=bottom, (C)=center, (L)=left, (R)=right
Photo Researchers, 36, 37, 60, 61, 90, 91, 102; Peter Arnold, Inc., 103; Tom Stack & Associates, 104; Tony Stone Images, 105; Photo Researchers, 106, 107; Tom Stack & Associates, 108-109; Peter Arnold,Inc, 109; Photo Researchers, 110-111, Photo Researchers, 112(1); Peter Arnold, Inc., 112(R); Tom Stack & Associates, 113(T); Tony Stone Images, 113(C); Peter Arnold, Inc., 113(B); Michael Campos Photography, 116, 117, 144, 145, 172, 173
All other photos by Harcourt Brace:
Larry Evans/Black Star; Walt Chyrnwski/Black Star; Todd Bigelow/Black Star; Joseph Rupp/Black Star; Santa Fabio/Black Star

### Illustration Credits

Leland Klanderman, Cover Art; Michael Grejniec, 4-11; Laura Ovresat, 12-31; Tracy Sabin, 36, 90-91, 116-117, 172-173; Daniel Moreton, 38-63; Joe Cepeda, 64-87; Doug Bowles, 88-89; Joung Un Kim, 92-103; Doug Cushman, 108-109, 112-113; Russ Willms, 118-145; Wong Herbert Yee, 146-159; Keith Baker, 160-171